WIND

BY HARRIET BRUNDLE

Weather Explorers

Weather
Explorers

©2016
Book Life
King's Lynn
Norfolk
PE30 4LS

ISBN: 978-1-910512-73-9

Written by:
Harriet Brundle
Edited by:
Gemma McMullen
Designed by:
Matt Rumbelow

A catalogue record for this book
is available from the British Library.

Renewa
by interr
in pers
by p

CONTENTS

Words in **bold** can be found in the glossary on page 24.

WIND

Wind is air that is moving around planet Earth.

Wind is sometimes a soft breeze, or it can be very strong and powerful.

SOFT BREEZE

HOW DOES WIND HAPPEN?

Some parts of the planet are very warm. Other parts do not get as much sunlight and so they are colder.

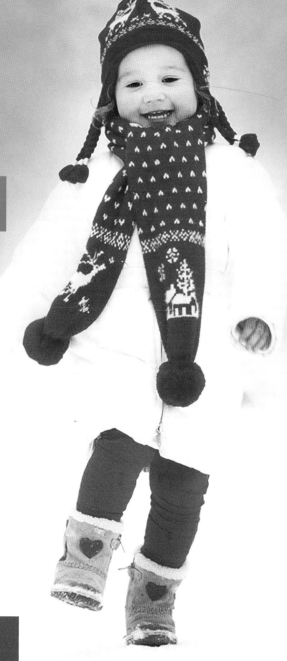

COLD PLACE

WARM PLACE

The air that is warmer rises up and the colder air **replaces** it. This causes wind.

COLD AIR

WARM AIR

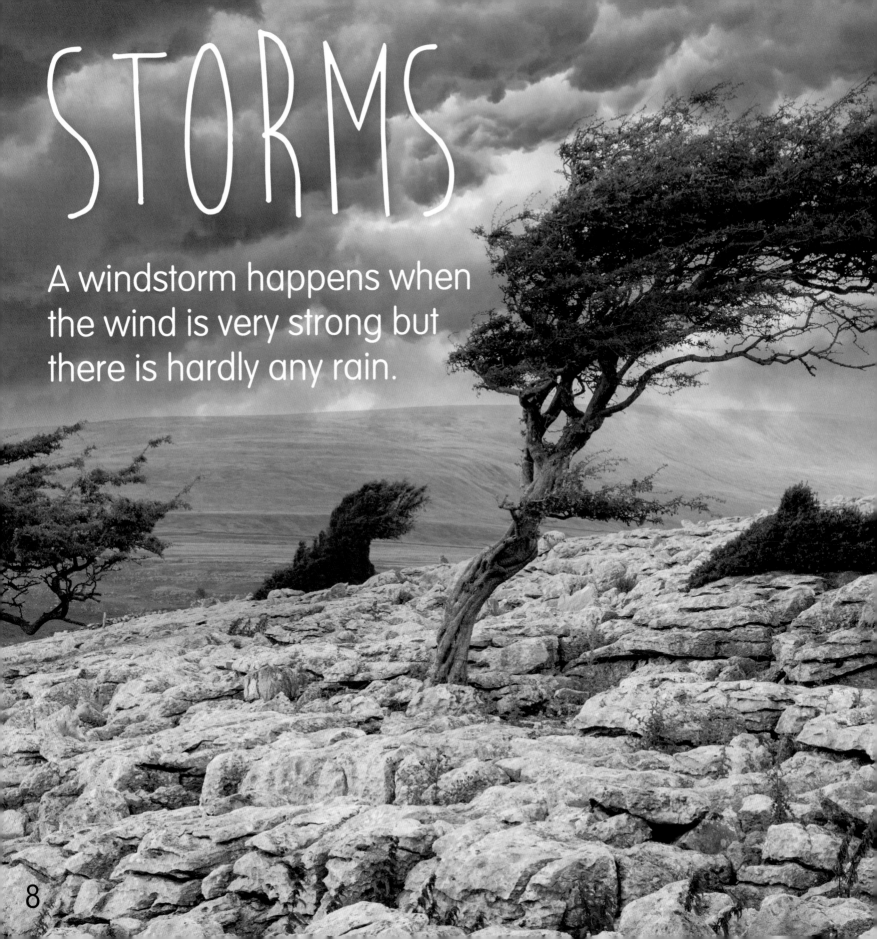

STORMS

A windstorm happens when the wind is very strong but there is hardly any rain.

When there is a thunderstorm, there will usually be strong winds and rain.

LIGHTNING

WIND AND THE SEASONS

There are four seasons in a year.

SPRING

SUMMER

WINTER

AUTUMN

It is most windy in autumn and winter when the weather is colder.

There is often wind in the other seasons too.

When the weather is warm in the summertime, the wind helps to keep us cool.

WHAT DO WE WEAR?

The wind can be very cold, so we wear our coats to keep warm.

We cannot wear a hat when it is windy.
The wind will blow it away!

PLANTS

Wind can **damage** plants by breaking off their branches, leaves or flowers.

FLOWER

SEEDS

Wind can be helpful to plants. The wind blows seeds from plants to new places. The seeds land on the ground and start to grow too.

ANIMALS

When the weather is windy, animals can find it difficult to hear.

Birds use the wind to glide when they are flying. This means they don't need to flap their wings as much, which helps them to save energy.

GLIDING

DANGEROUS WIND

Some types of wind can be very dangerous. A hurricane is a very strong storm with fast wind and heavy rain.

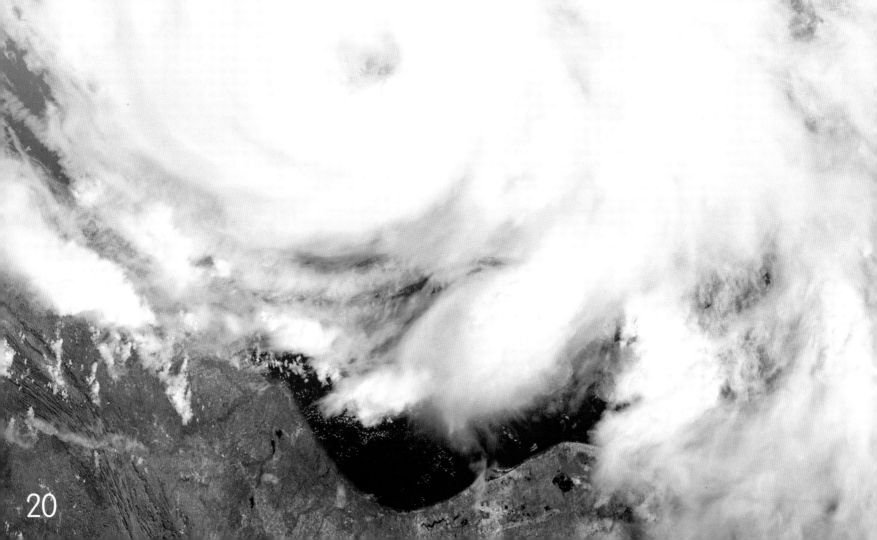

A tornado is wind that has become **funnel** shaped and moves across the ground.

THE STRONGEST TORNADOES CAN KNOCK DOWN BUILDINGS.

DID YOU KNOW?

People have used the wind to sail around the Earth. The fastest ever attempt took just 57 days.

THE SPEED OF THE WIND CAN BE **MEASURED** IN "KNOTS".

In some places on Earth, the wind can reach speeds faster than a racing car!